Copyright © 2021 Anna Nadler
All rights reserved
Published by Little Birdie Press™
No part of this publication may be
reproduced, stored in a retrieval system or
transmitted in any form or by any means,
electronic, mechanical, photocopying, recording
or otherwise, without prior written permission
from the author/publisher.
www.annanadler.com

Table of Contents

p.4-5 - About the author
p.6-7 - Introduction
p.8-9 - How to use this book
p.10-11 - Line types and shading techniques
p.12-13 - Drawing animal features and practice
p.14-15 - Drawing animal features and practice
p.16-17 - Drawing a DOG and practice
p.18-19 - Drawing a DOG and practice
p.20-21 - Drawing a CAT and practice
p.22-23 - Drawing a CAT and practice
p.24-25 - Drawing a BOAR and practice
p.26-27 - Drawing a BOAR and practice
p.28-29 - Drawing a FISH and practice
p.30-31 - Drawing a FISH and practice
p.32-33 - Drawing a PARROT and practice
p.34-35 - Drawing a PARROT and practice
p.36-37 - Drawing a RABBIT and practice
p.38-39 - Drawing a RABBIT and practice
p.40-41 - Drawing a LION and practice
p.42-43 - Drawing a LION and practice
p.44-45 - Drawing a STINGRAY and practice
p.46-47 - Drawing a STINGRAY and practice
p.48-49 - Drawing a BEAR and practice
p.50-51 - Drawing a BEAR and practice
p.52-53 - Drawing a GOOSE and practice
p.54-55 - Drawing a GOOSE and practice

Table of Contents

p.56-57 - Drawing an ANTELOPE and practice
p.58-59 - Drawing an ANTELOPE and practice
p.60-61 - Drawing an ELEPHANT and practice
p.62-63 - Drawing an ELEPHANT and practice
p.64-65 - Drawing a GIRAFFE and practice
p.66-67 - Drawing a GIRAFFE and practice
p.68-69 - Drawing a GOAT and practice
p.70-71 - Drawing a GOAT and practice
p.72-73 - Drawing a ZEBRA and practice
p.74-75 - Drawing a ZEBRA and practice
p.76-77 - Drawing a SNAKE and practice
p.78-79 - Drawing a SNAKE and practice
p.80-81 - Drawing a RHINO and practice
p.82-83 - Drawing a RHINO and practice
p.84-85 - Drawing a PEACOCK and practice
p.86-87 - Drawing a PEACOCK and practice
p.88-89 - Drawing a OSTRICH and practice
p.90-91 - Drawing a OSTRICH and practice
p.92-93 - Drawing a MONKEY and practice
p.94-95 - Drawing a MONKEY and practice
p.96-97 - Drawing a LLAMA and practice
p.98-99 - Drawing a LLAMA and practice
p.100-101 - Drawing a LEOPARD and practice
p.102-103 - Drawing a LEOPARD and practice
p.104-105 - Drawing a KANGAROO and practice
p.106-107 - Drawing a KANGAROO and practice
p.108-109 - Final note and more of our series
p.110-147 - Drawing practice pages

Anna Nadler is a book illustrator who lives and works in New York City. She has been drawing since the age of two - it's been her life-long passion and career for several decades. Anna has taught both kids and adults how to draw, and has finally decided to put some of that knowledge into a simple and comprehensive book for everyone to benefit.

Anna loves to draw people, places, animals, architecture and nature. She goes out to draw from life any chance she gets. You can find many of her coloring books, children's books, journals and more on Amazon.

Dear Artist,

Thank you for getting the "How To Draw Animals!" volume! This book will teach you animal drawing tips using the method of observation, because in order to really achieve realistic animal drawings, you need to learn their anatomy, at least from a visual perspective. How do we do that? By observing them in real life, videos and photos.

While this book gives you a solid set of animal drawings to practice on, with corresponding steps to show the drawing progress, it is just the beginning to get you started on your own journey.

In order to understand how to draw animals in a realistic way, we first must understand that all living creatures have a skeleton underneath their bodies.

Each species and subspecies have varied kinds of skeletons. We don't necessarily need to draw the skeleton, however we must "feel" it when we draw, so our drawings have substance and structure and our animals' paws, wings and necks don't bend like they are made of rubber.

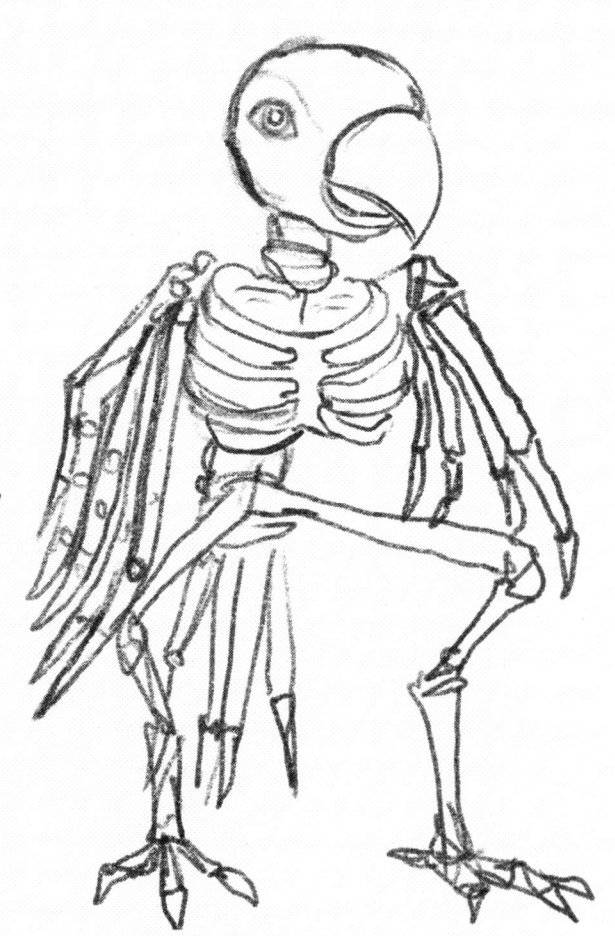

Therefore, it is necessary to comprehend the anatomy of animals in order to be able to draw them realistically.

The best way to do this is by observation. Take a trip to the zoo and sketch! If you have a domestic animal, like a bird, fish, dog or cat, even a snake or a frog, use them as models.

If you don't have any animals at home or cannot go to the zoo, watch some videos on-line featuring animals to understand how the anatomy is structured. You can also use photos, after having watched videos to see how legs, tails, wings bend and fold.

To sum it up, this book is a guide for you to learn to problem solve and draw on your own! The more you draw, the better you will become. You can always use this book as a quick reference guide.

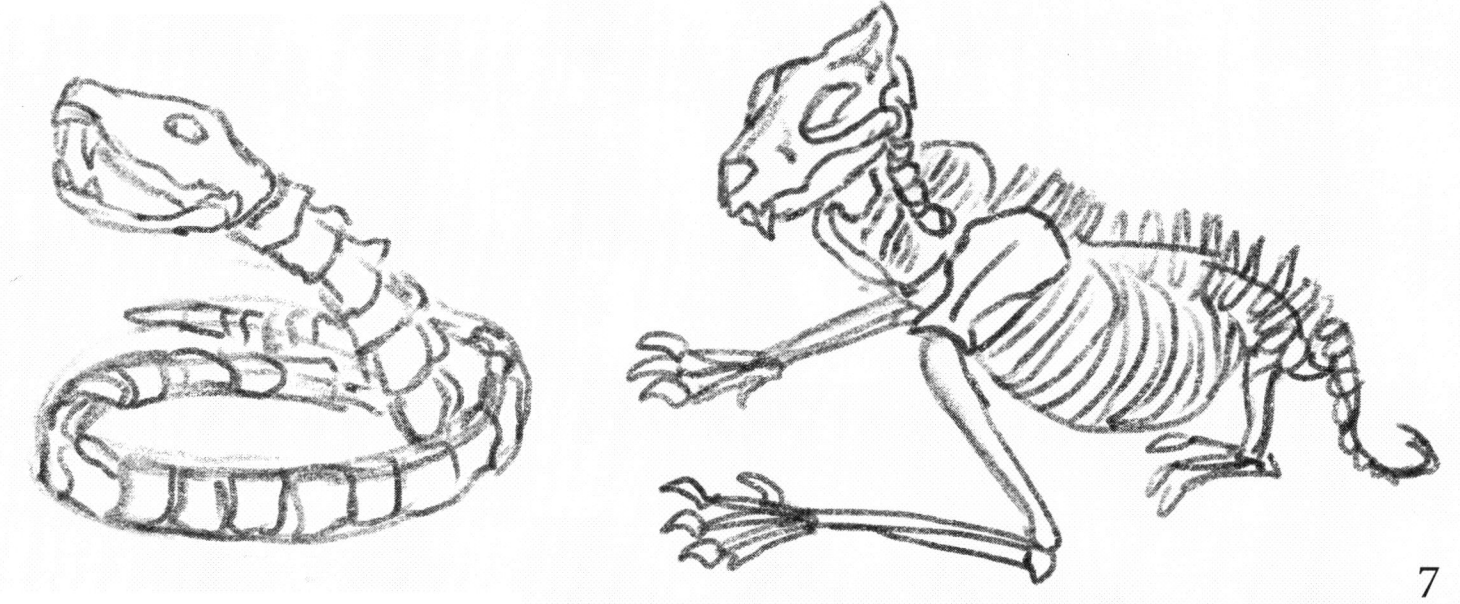

How to use this book

Once you have understood that we are always seeing our animals as three dimentional beings that have skeleton and muscles under their skin, we can start to practice.

While working on this book, I went out to the zoo and took lots of animal photos. I recommend that after you are finished with this book, you do the same. Having your own references is a great way to learn drawing, rather than just using other people's drawings alone. I have included photos in this book for a reason. So that you can also use photos for your references, not just drawings.

To help guide your drawing process, each animal in this book has five steps to develop its drawing. The easiest way to start is to indicate the head of the animal. Using a pencil, draw the head as you see it, make sure to leave enough room on your paper for the rest of the body.

Once you sketch out the head, you can add an outline of the body, then add limbs and a tail or wings, etc.

Step 1   Step 2   Step 3

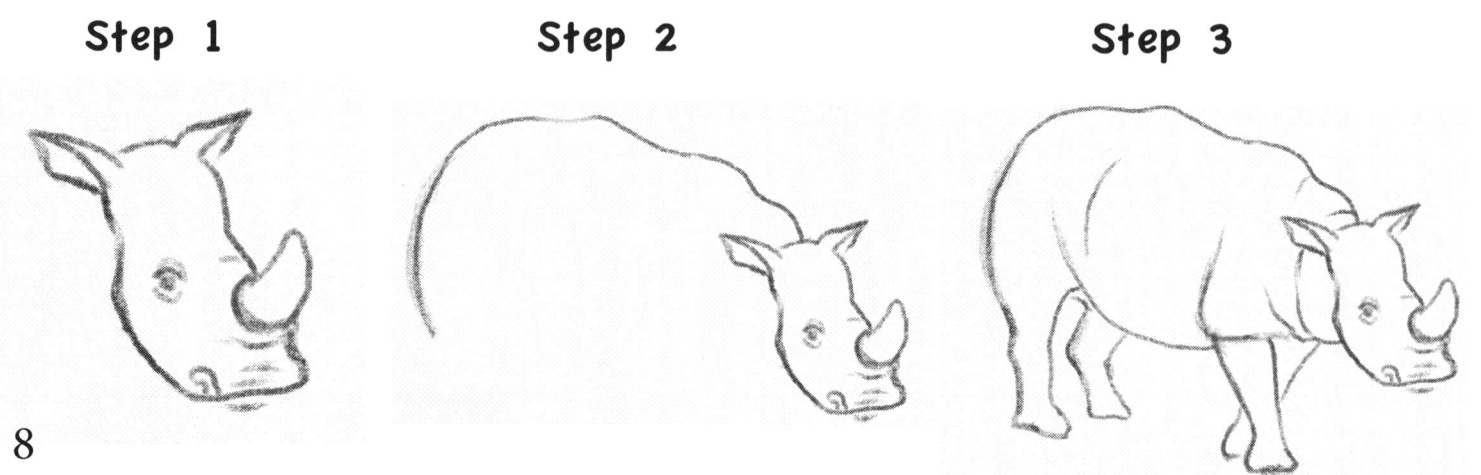

After this step, you have two options, which can be used alone or together. I recommend picking either step four or step five. Each of those steps adds detail, or realism in a different way.

Step four adds shading using a soft pencil or a charcoal, and step five adds detail using a pen or a marker.

Step 4

There are different methods for shading and crosshatching. The best way to do this is by following the shape of the animal's body. Do not randomly shade as if you were shading on a board or a floor. These are 3D creatures, that each have its own unique shape.

Step 5

So when you shade or crosshatch, make sure to use lines that follow the animal's shape, as if you were drawing directly on the animal. Usually, we would use the darker or more concentrated shading and crosshatching in darker parts and less of it in the more lit parts. Observe the example drawings for an idea of where to shade.

For practice, replicate the example drawings on the corresponding opposite pages. You can either draw each step separately or make one whole animal drawing at once. The steps are simply there to show you the breakdown. Do what is comfortable for you. These pages are there for you to practice and improve your skills.

In these two pages, let's talk about some basic line types as well as basic shading techniques.

Below you can see various types of lines and markings, using various art materials.

Pencil: Used for the initial sketch and shading.

Charcoal: Used for drawing and shading

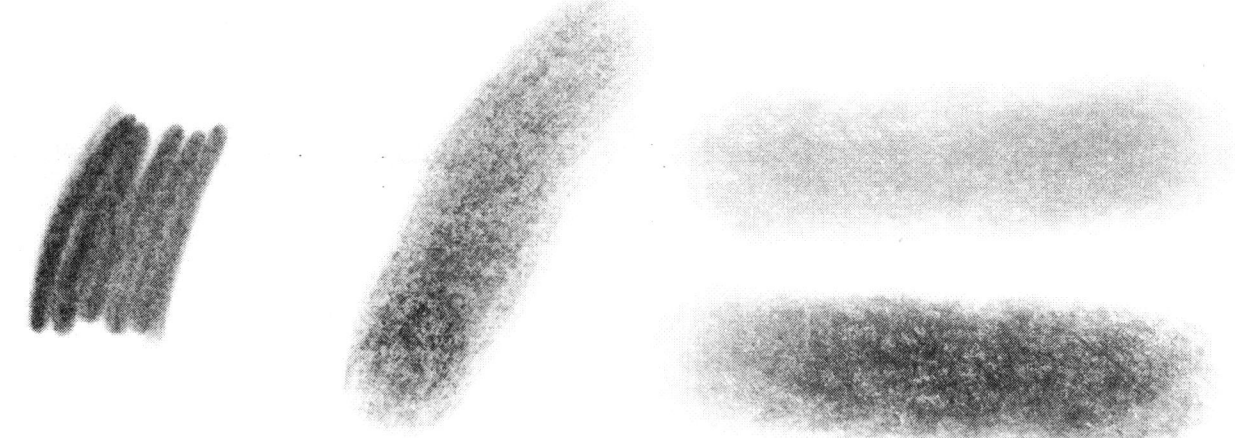

Pen & Ink: Used to draw and to show details

Shading and Cross-hatching lines.

Sometimes we can add shading or crosshatching to our drawings to show more detail or realism. When doing it, follow the shape and form of the object.

1. Simple shading using charcoal or a soft pencil.

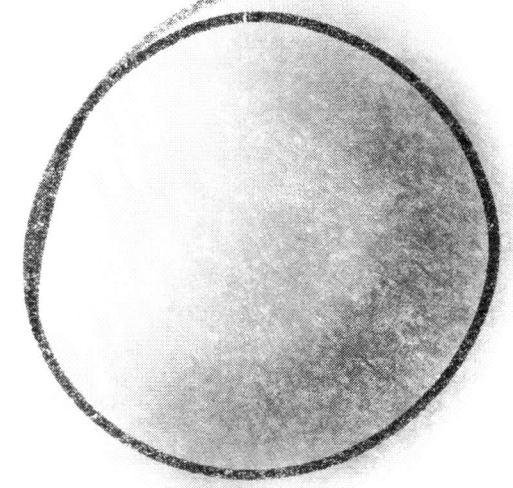

2. Pen and ink shading on the side is added following the shape.

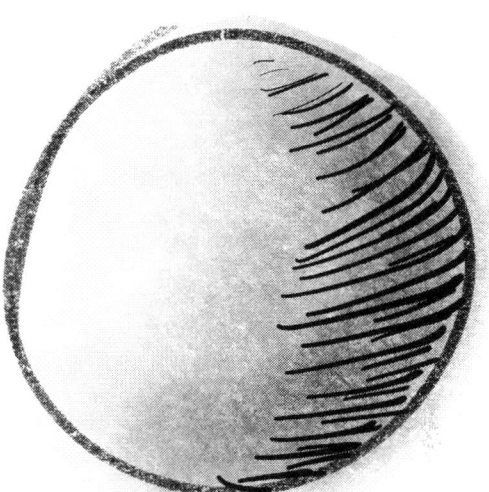

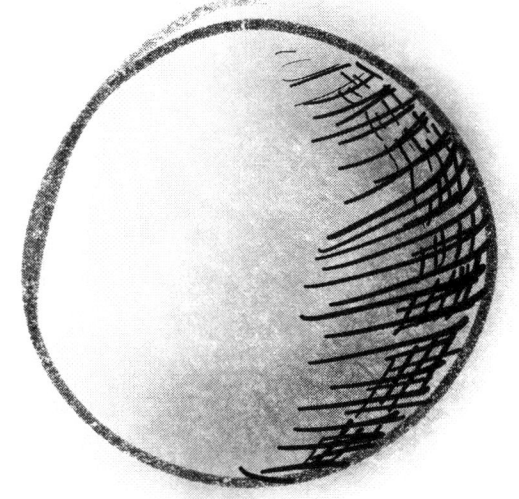

3.

Crosshatching lines are added to show a darker shading gradation.

Drawing animals and their features.

Eyes: When you draw eyes, make sure the eyes sit inside the eye sockets. This can be achieved with simple indicator lines.

Noses & Snouts: Practice drawing a variety of animal noses, front and side views. Pay attention to the way many different animals' noses differ from one another.

12

Practice Page

Look at the page on the left. Practice drawing the animal parts you see there in the box below.

13

Drawing paws, legs, wings, fins & tails.

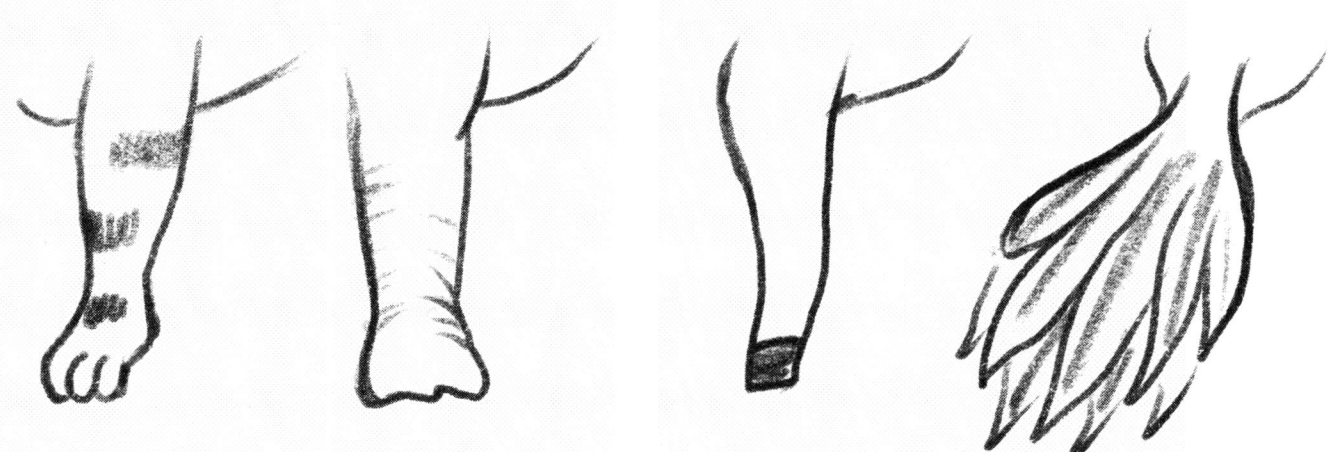

When drawing legs, show them as they are in the front of the body, with lines coming out of/overlapping the body.

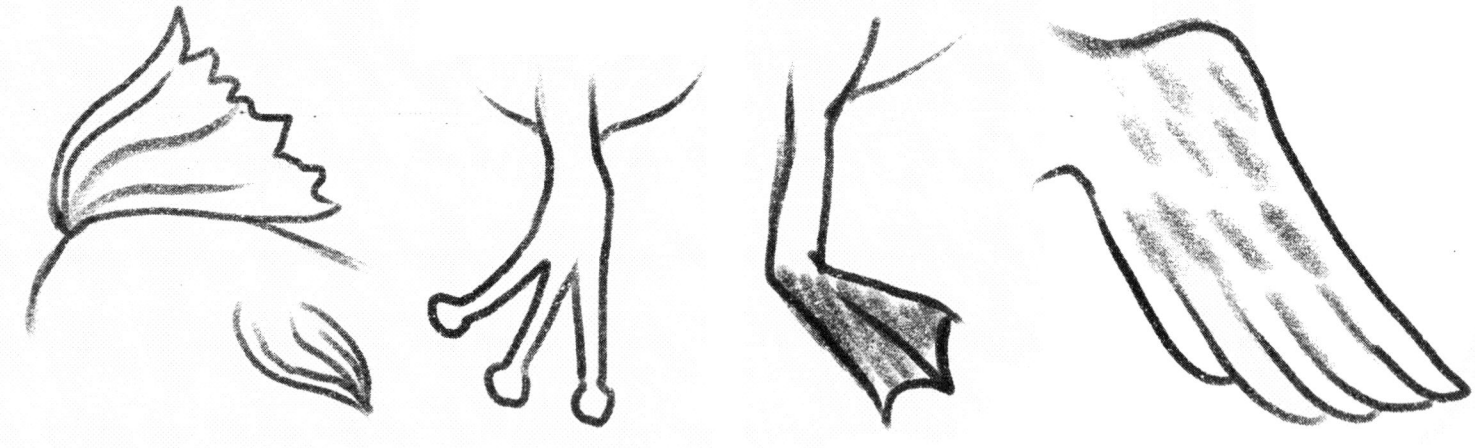

Show joints and folds with simple lines and shading. Pay attention to different animal species' variety of limbs and tails.

Practice Page

Look at the page on the left. Practice drawing the animal parts you see there in the box below.

DOG

1. Draw the dog's head.

3. Finish the drawing by adding the rest of the body and legs.

2. Add an outline of the body.

16

Practice Page

Look at the page on the left. Draw the animal in the frame below, by following the steps listed.

DOG

The next steps can be used interchangeably to show more realism and detail in your drawings. We recommend using either one or the other. However sometimes you can combine the two. Step 4 shows shading done with charcoal or pencil, Step 5 shows adding detail using a pen or a brush.

5. You can also add details with a pen, indicating fur and details with strokes and crosshatching.

4. Add shading and detail.

18

Practice Page

Look at the page on the left. Draw the animal in the frame below, by following the steps listed.

CAT

1. Draw the cat's head.

2. Add an outline of the body.

3. Finish the drawing by adding legs and a tail.

Practice Page

Look at the page on the left. Draw the animal in the frame below, by following the steps listed.

CAT

The next steps can be used interchangeably to show more realism and detail in your drawings. We recommend using either one or the other. However sometimes you can combine the two. Step 4 shows shading done with charcoal or pencil, Step 5 shows adding detail using a pen or a brush.

5. You can also add details with a pen, indicating fur, whiskers, with strokes and crosshatching.

4. Add shading and detail.

Practice Page

Look at the page on the left. Draw the animal in the frame below, by following the steps listed.

BOAR

1. Draw the boar's head.

2. Add an outline of the body.

3. Finish the drawing by adding the rest of the body and a tail.

Practice Page

Look at the page on the left. Draw the animal in the frame below, by following the steps listed.

25

BOAR

The next steps can be used interchangeably to show more realism and detail in your drawings. We recommend using either one or the other. However sometimes you can combine the two. Step 4 shows shading done with charcoal or pencil. Step 5 shows adding detail using a pen or a brush.

4. Add shading and detail.

5. You can also add details with a pen, indicating hair and texture, with strokes and crosshatching.

Practice Page

Look at the page on the left. Draw the animal in the frame below, by following the steps listed.

FISH

1. Draw the fish's head.

2. Add an outline of the body.

3. Finish the drawing by adding the rest of the body and a tail.

Practice Page

Look at the page on the left. Draw the animal in the frame below, by following the steps listed.

FISH

The next steps can be used interchangeably to show more realism and detail in your drawings. We recommend using either one or the other. However sometimes you can combine the two. Step 4 shows shading done with charcoal or pencil, Step 5 shows adding detail using a pen or a brush.

4. Add shading and detail.

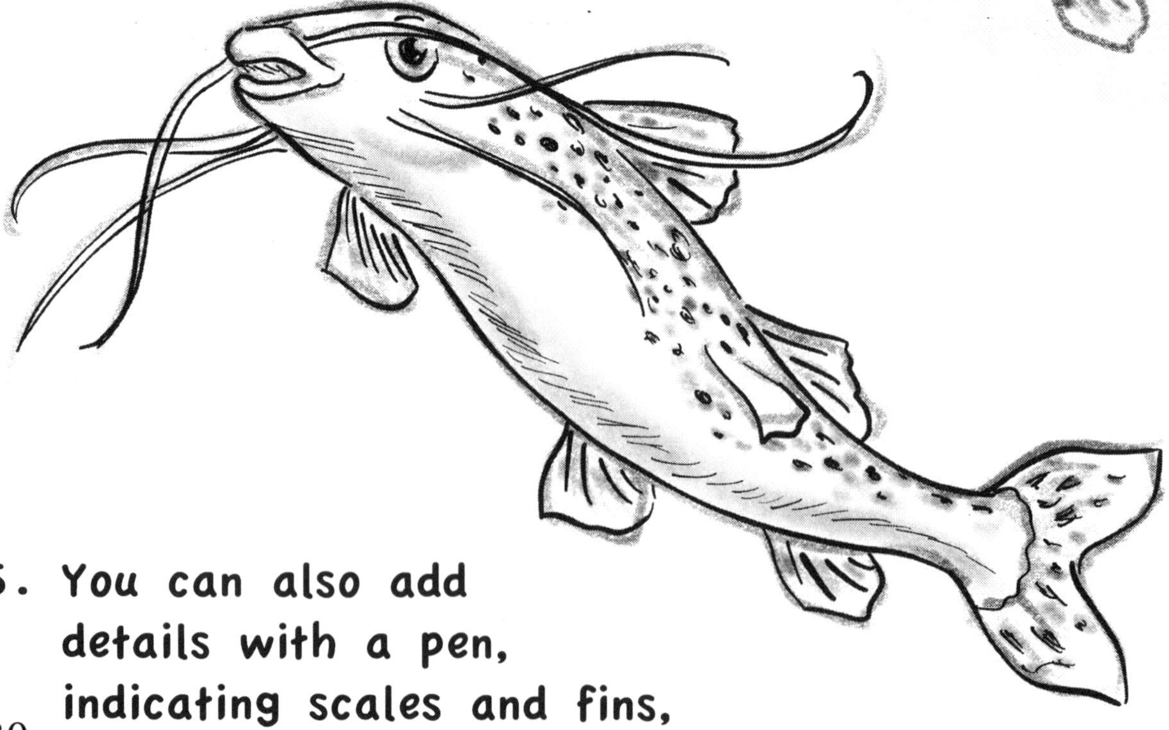

5. You can also add details with a pen, indicating scales and fins, with strokes and crosshatching.

30

Practice Page

Look at the page on the left. Draw the animal in the frame below, by following the steps listed.

PARROT

1. Draw the bird's head.

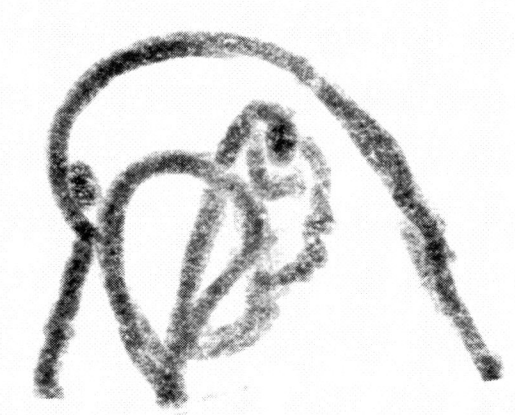

2. Add an outline of the body.

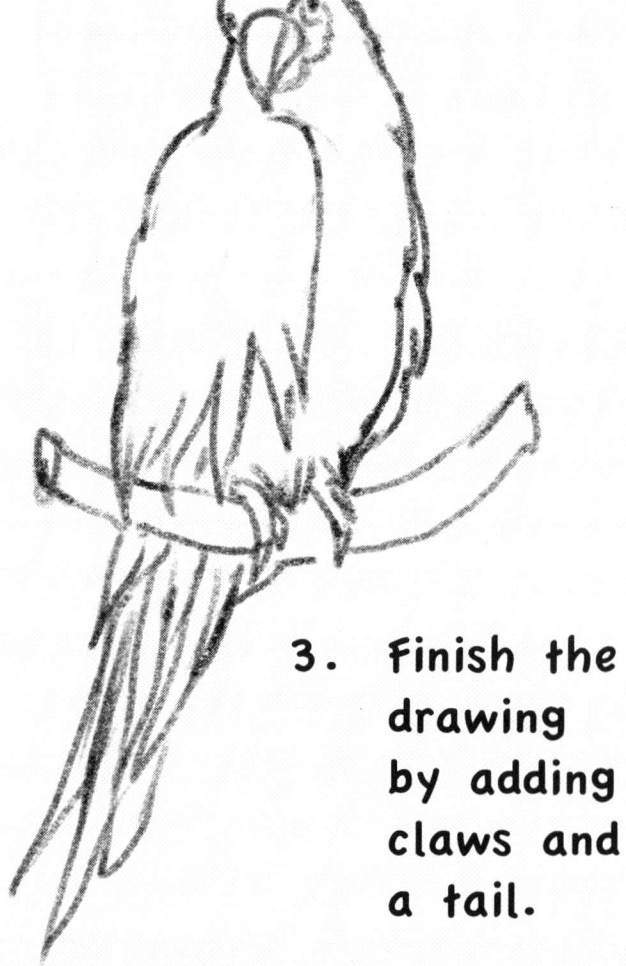

3. Finish the drawing by adding claws and a tail.

Practice Page

Look at the page on the left. Draw the animal in the frame below, by following the steps listed.

PARROT

The next steps can be used interchangeably to show more realism and detail in your drawings. We recommend using either one or the other. However sometimes you can combine the two. Step 4 shows shading done with charcoal or pencil, Step 5 shows adding detail using a pen or a brush.

4. Add shading and detail.

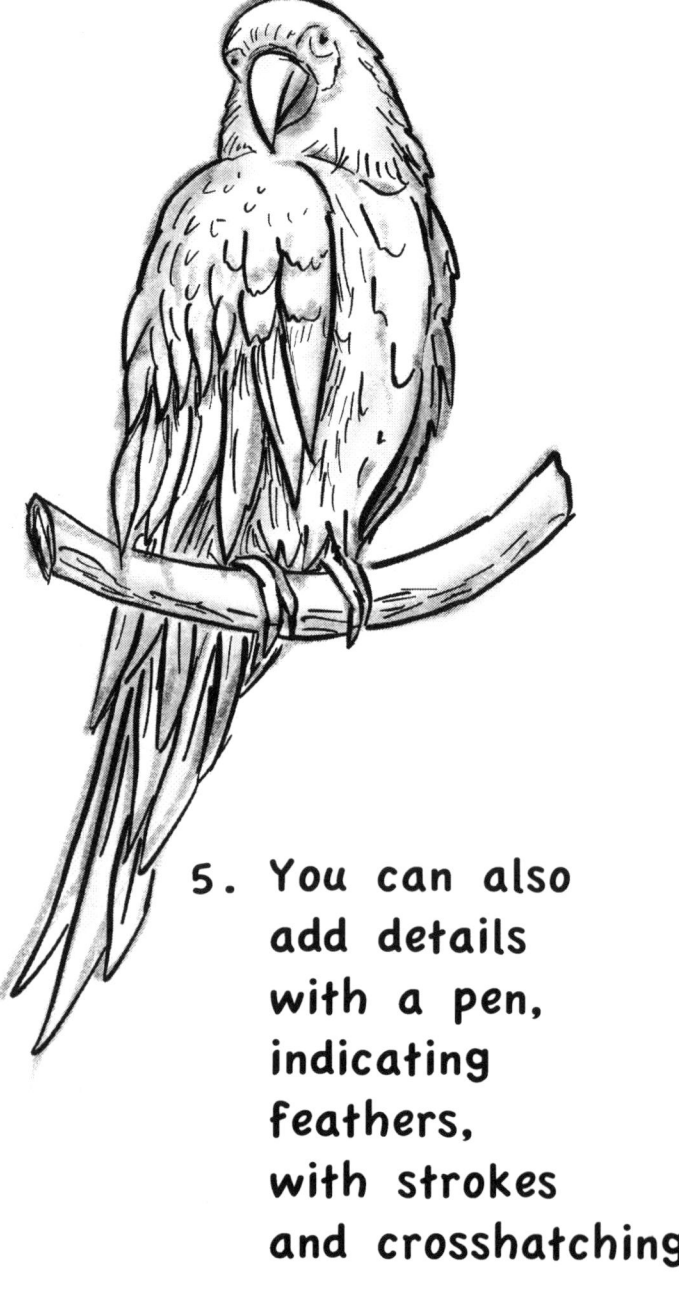

5. You can also add details with a pen, indicating feathers, with strokes and crosshatching.

Practice Page

Look at the page on the left. Draw the animal in the frame below, by following the steps listed.

RABBIT

1. Draw the rabbit's head.

2. Add an outline of the body.

3. Finish the drawing by adding the rest of the body and legs.

36

Practice Page

Look at the page on the left. Draw the animal in the frame below, by following the steps listed.

RABBIT

The next steps can be used interchangeably to show more realism and detail in your drawings. We recommend using either one or the other. However sometimes you can combine the two. Step 4 shows shading done with charcoal or pencil, Step 5 shows adding detail using a pen or a brush.

4. Add shading and detail.

5. You can also add details with a pen, indicating hair and texture, with strokes and crosshatching.

Practice Page

Look at the page on the left. Draw the animal in the frame below, by following the steps listed.

LION

1. Draw the lion's head.

2. Add an outline of the body.

3. Finish the drawing by adding the rest of the body and a tail.

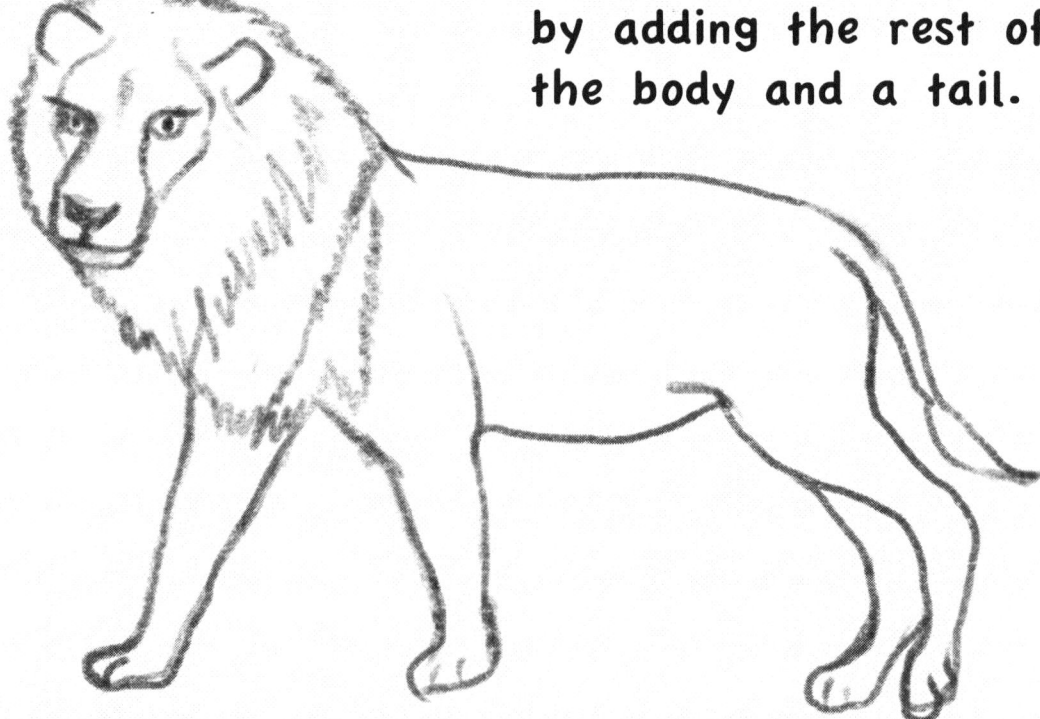

Practice Page

Look at the page on the left. Draw the animal in the frame below, by following the steps listed.

LION

The next steps can be used interchangeably to show more realism and detail in your drawings. It is simpler to use either one or the other. However sometimes you can combine the two. Step 4 shows shading done with charcoal or pencil, Step 5 shows adding detail using a pen or a brush.

4. Add shading and detail.

5. You can also add details with a pen, indicating hair and texture with strokes and cross-hatching.

Practice Page

Look at the page on the left. Draw the animal in the frame below, by following the steps listed.

STINGRAY

1. Draw the stingray's head.

2. Add an outline of the body.

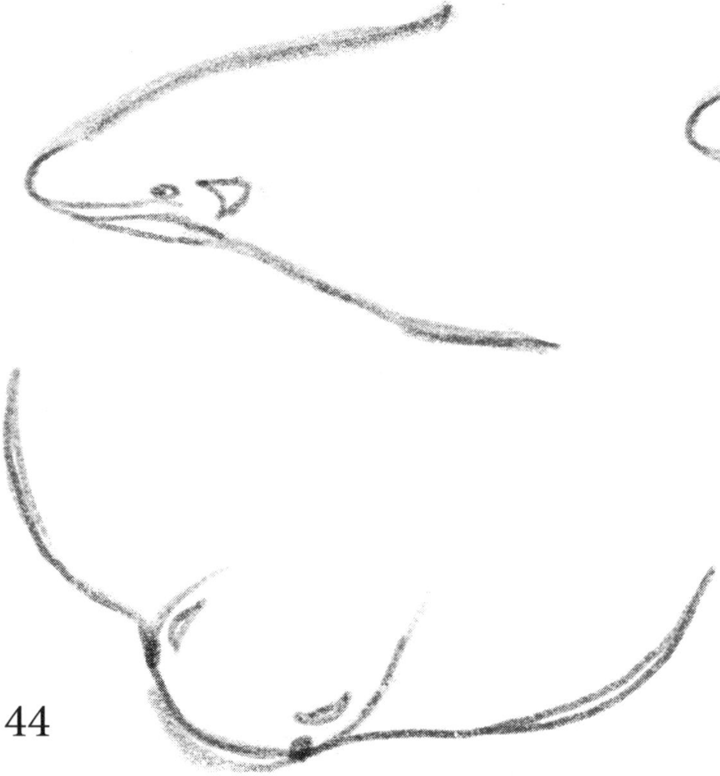

3. Finish the drawing by adding the rest of the body and a tail.

Practice Page

Look at the page on the left. Draw the animal in the frame below, by following the steps listed.

STINGRAY

The next steps can be used interchangeably to show more realism and detail in your drawings. We recommend using either one or the other. However sometimes you can combine the two. Step 4 shows shading done with charcoal or pencil, Step 5 shows adding detail using a pen or a brush.

5. You can also add details with a pen, indicating texture and fins, with strokes and crosshatching.

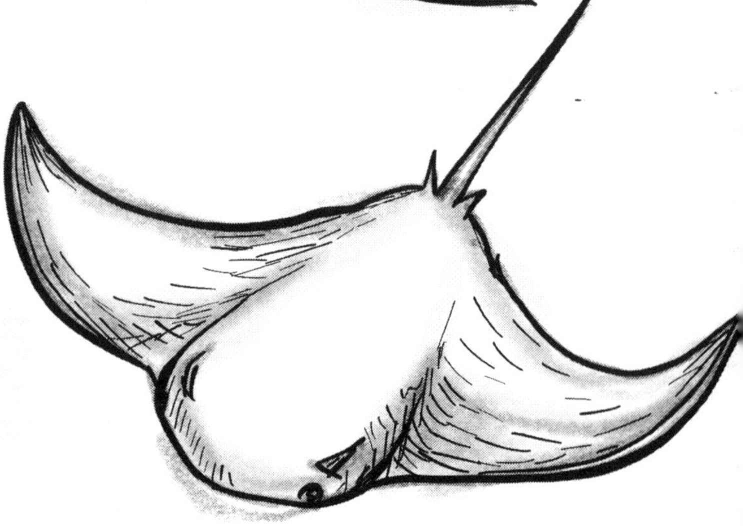

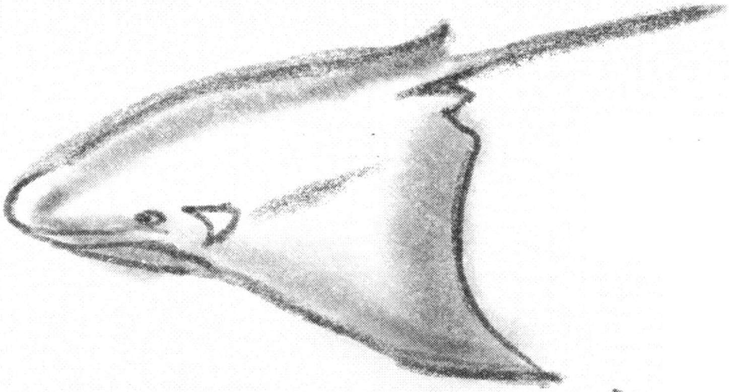

4. Add shading and detail.

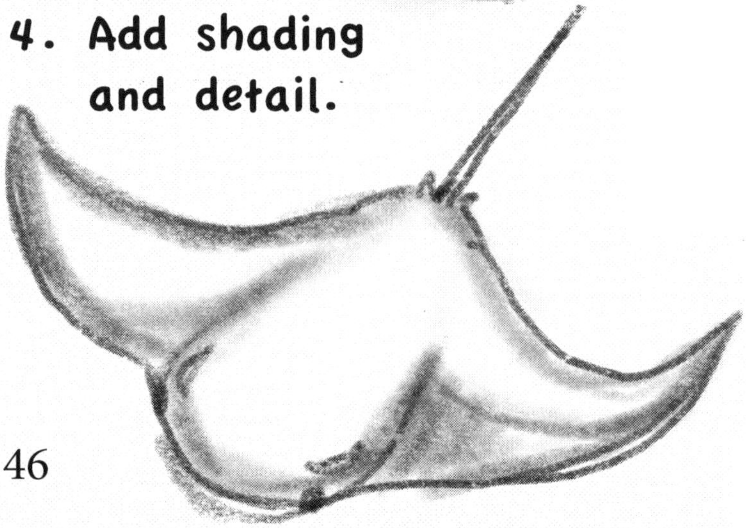

Practice Page

Look at the page on the left. Draw the animal in the frame below, by following the steps listed.

BEAR

1. Draw the bear's head.

3. Finish the drawing by adding the rest of the body and legs.

2. Add an outline of the body.

Practice Page

Look at the page on the left. Draw the animal in the frame below, by following the steps listed.

BEAR

The next steps can be used interchangeably to show more realism and detail in your drawings. We recommend using either one or the other. However sometimes you can combine the two. Step 4 shows shading done with charcoal or pencil, Step 5 shows adding detail using a pen or a brush.

4. Add shading and detail.

5. You can also add details with a pen, indicating hair and texture, with strokes and crosshatching.

Practice Page

Look at the page on the left. Draw the animal in the frame below, by following the steps listed.

GOOSE

1. Draw the goose's head.

2. Add an outline of the body.

3. Finish the drawing by adding the rest of the body and a tail.

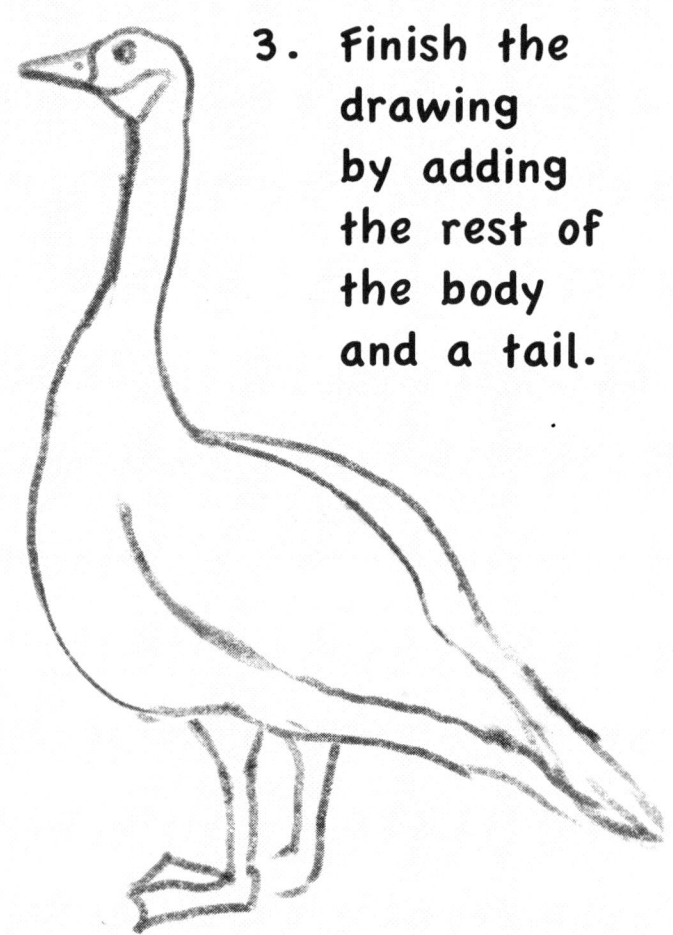

Practice Page

Look at the page on the left. Draw the animal in the frame below, by following the steps listed.

53

GOOSE

The next steps can be used interchangeably to show more realism and detail in your drawings. We recommend using either one or the other. However sometimes you can combine the two. Step 4 shows shading done with charcoal or pencil, Step 5 shows adding detail using a pen or a brush.

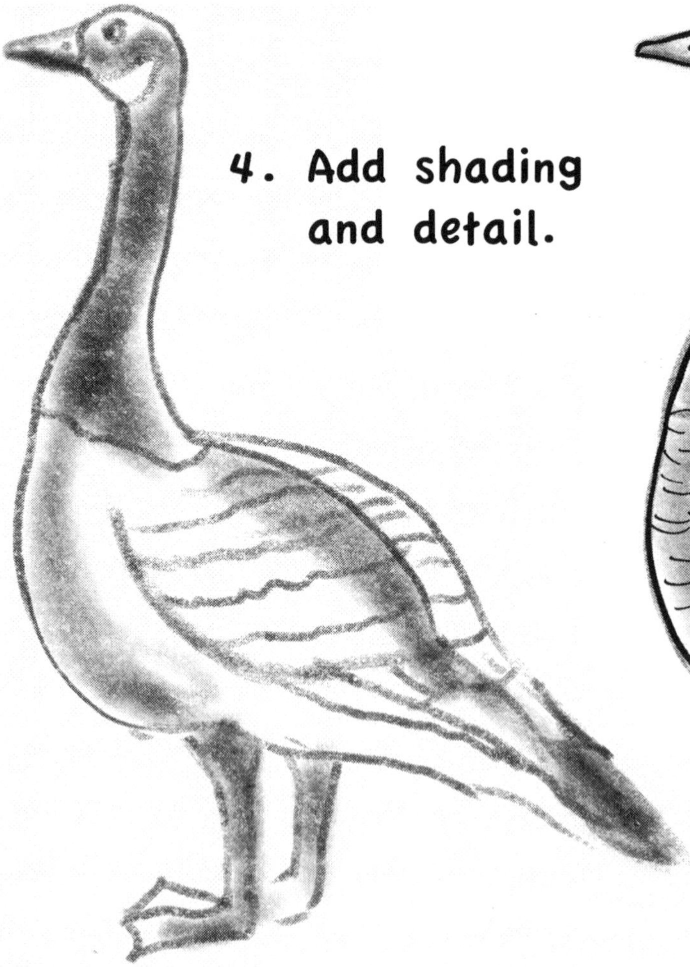

4. Add shading and detail.

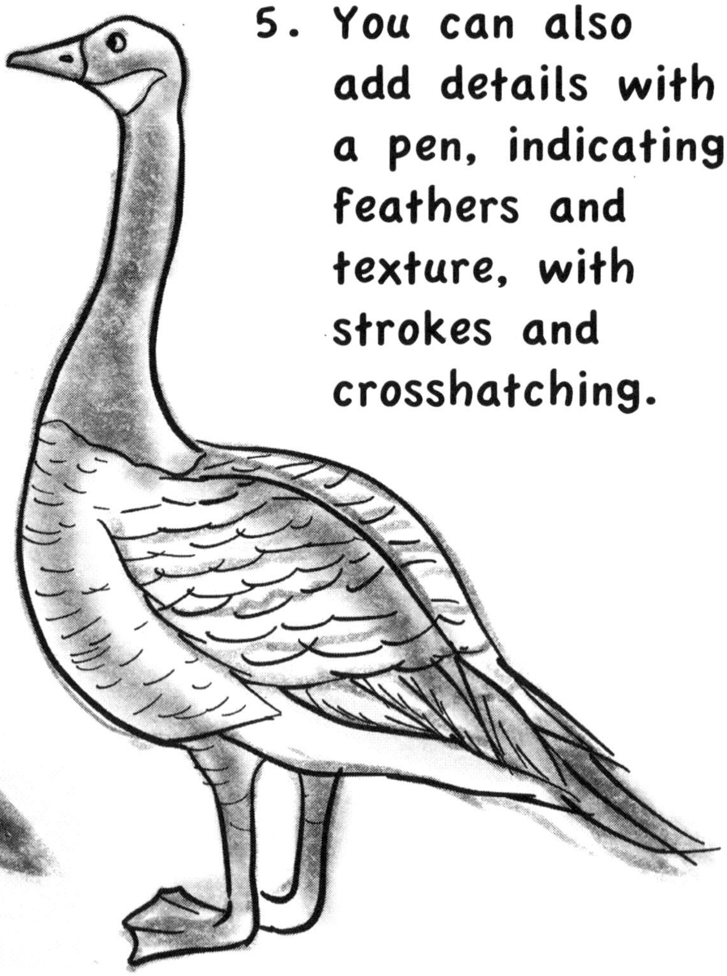

5. You can also add details with a pen, indicating feathers and texture, with strokes and crosshatching.

Practice Page

Look at the page on the left. Draw the animal in the frame below, by following the steps listed.

ANTELOPE

1. Draw the antelope's head.

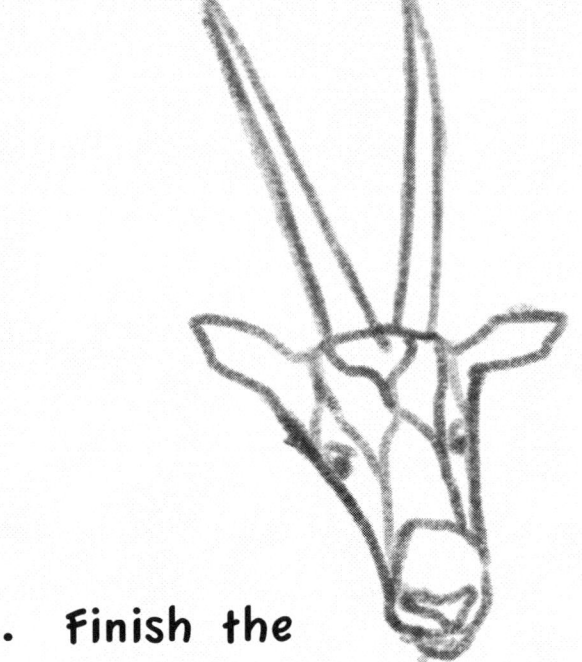

2. Add an outline of the body.

3. Finish the drawing by adding the rest of the body and legs.

Practice Page

Look at the page on the left. Draw the animal in the frame below, by following the steps listed.

ANTELOPE

The next steps can be used interchangeably to show more realism and detail in your drawings. We recommend using either one or the other. However sometimes you can combine the two. Step 4 shows shading done with charcoal or pencil, Step 5 shows adding detail using a pen or a brush.

5. You can also add details with a pen, indicating hair and details with strokes and crosshatching.

4. Add shading and detail.

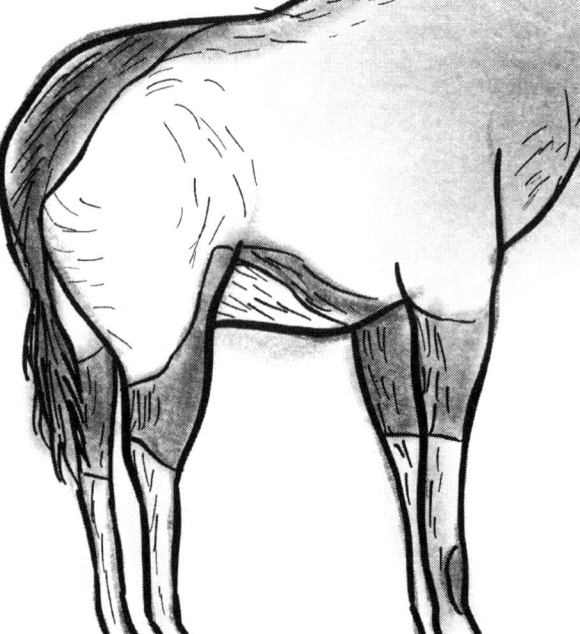

Practice Page

Look at the page on the left. Draw the animal in the frame below, by following the steps listed.

ELEPHANT

1. Draw the elephant's head.

2. Add an outline of the body.

3. Finish the drawing by adding the rest of the body and legs.

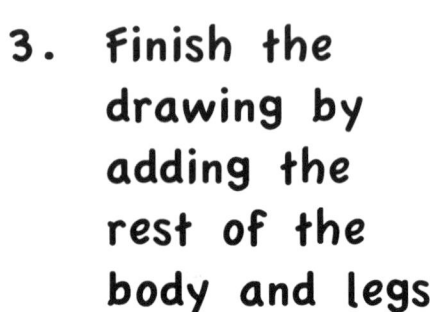

Practice Page

Look at the page on the left. Draw the animal in the frame below, by following the steps listed.

ELEPHANT

The next steps can be used interchangeably to show more realism and detail in your drawings. We recommend using either one or the other. However sometimes you can combine the two. Step 4 shows shading done with charcoal or pencil, Step 5 shows adding detail using a pen or a brush.

4. Add shading and detail.

5. You can also add details with a pen, indicating skin texture with strokes and crosshatching.

Practice Page

Look at the page on the left. Draw the animal in the frame below, by following the steps listed.

GIRAFFE

1. Draw the giraffe's head.

2. Add an outline of the body.

3. Finish the drawing by adding the rest of the body and legs.

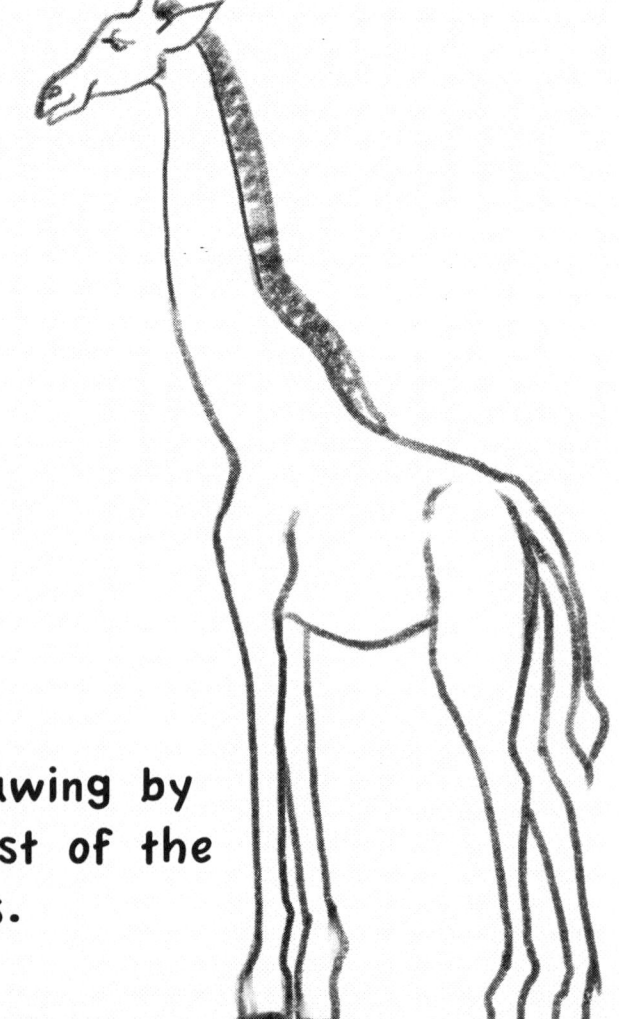

Practice Page

Look at the page on the left. Draw the animal in the frame below, by following the steps listed.

GIRAFFE

The next steps can be used interchangeably to show more realism and detail in your drawings. We recommend using either one or the other. However sometimes you can combine the two. Step 4 shows shading done with charcoal or pencil, Step 5 shows adding detail using a pen or a brush.

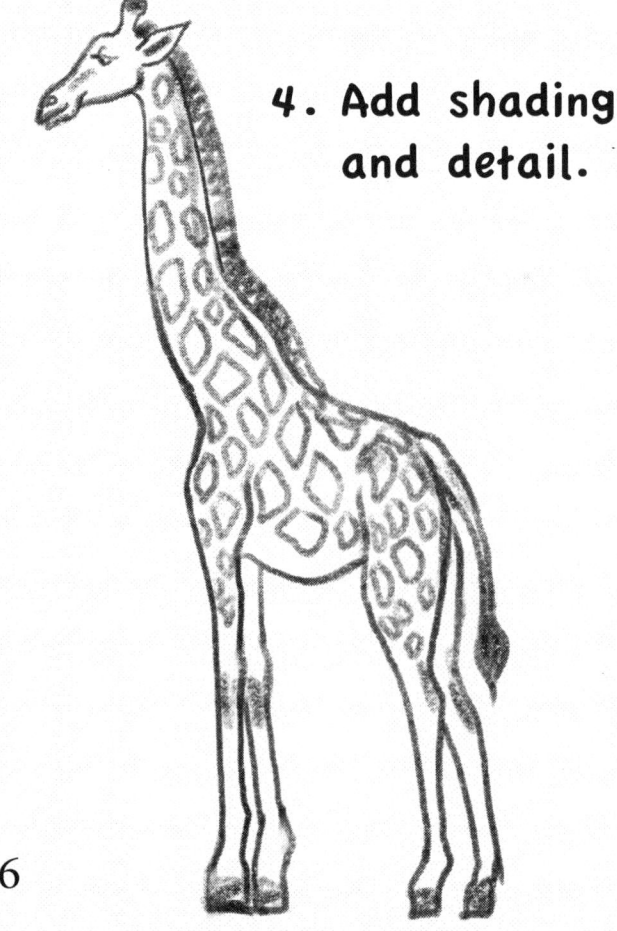

4. Add shading and detail.

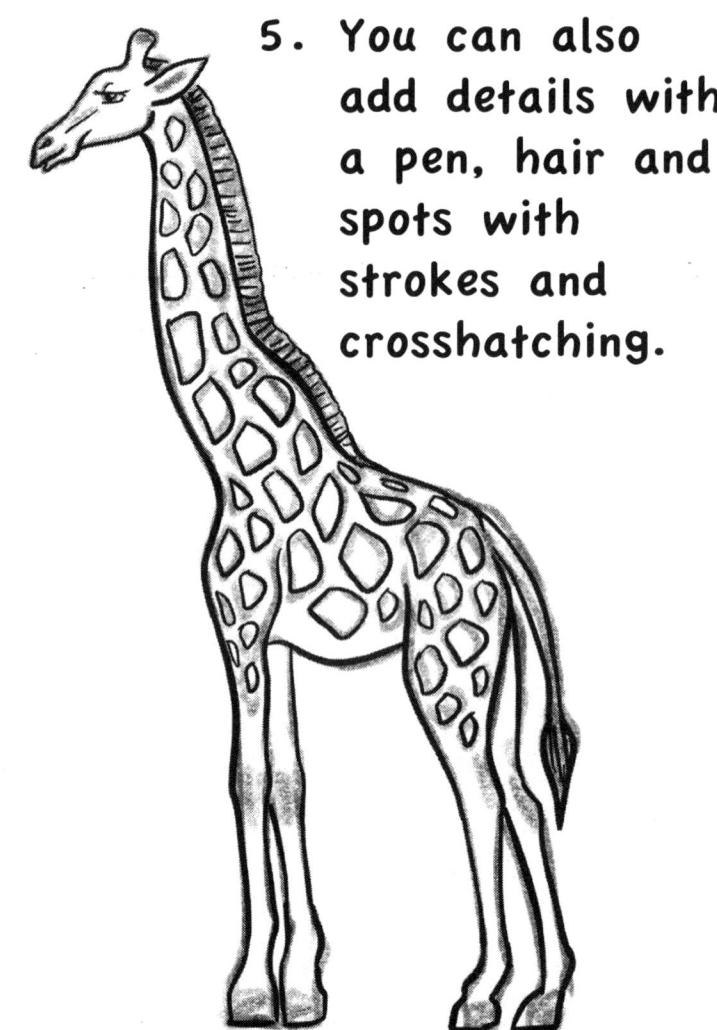

5. You can also add details with a pen, hair and spots with strokes and crosshatching.

Practice Page

Look at the page on the left. Draw the animal in the frame below, by following the steps listed.

GOAT

1. Draw the goat's head.

2. Add an outline of the body.

3. Finish the drawing by adding the rest of the body and legs.

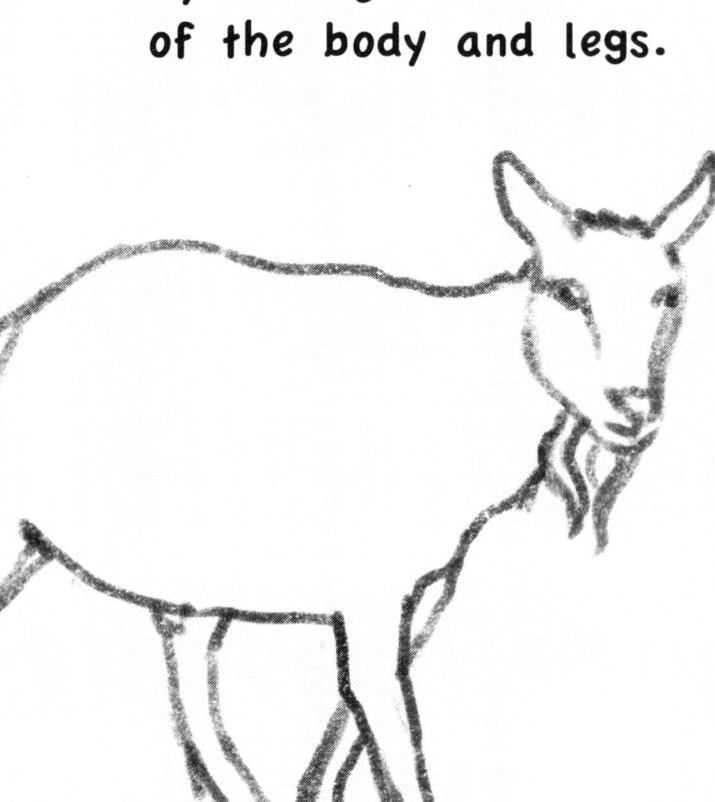

68

Practice Page

Look at the page on the left. Draw the animal in the frame below, by following the steps listed.

GOAT

The next steps can be used interchangeably to show more realism and detail in your drawings. We recommend using either one or the other. However sometimes you can combine the two. Step 4 shows shading done with charcoal or pencil, Step 5 shows adding detail using a pen or a brush.

5. You can also add details with a pen, indicating hair and details, with strokes and crosshatching.

4. Add shading and detail.

Practice Page

Look at the page on the left. Draw the animal in the frame below, by following the steps listed.

ZEBRA

1. Draw the zebra's head.

2. Add an outline of the body.

3. Finish the drawing by adding the rest of the body and legs.

Practice Page

Look at the page on the left. Draw the animal in the frame below, by following the steps listed.

ZEBRA

The next steps can be used interchangeably to show more realism and detail in your drawings. We recommend using either one or the other. However sometimes you can combine the two. Step 4 shows shading done with charcoal or pencil, Step 5 shows adding detail using a pen or a brush.

4. Add shading and detail.

5. You can also add details with a pen, indicating hair and stripes with strokes and crosshatching.

Practice Page

Look at the page on the left. Draw the animal in the frame below, by following the steps listed.

SNAKE

1. Draw the snake's head.

2. Add an outline of the body.

3. Finish the drawing by adding the rest of the snake coils and a tail.

Practice Page

Look at the page on the left. Draw the animal in the frame below, by following the steps listed.

SNAKE

The next steps can be used interchangeably to show more realism and detail in your drawings. It is simpler to use either one or the other. However sometimes you can combine the two. Step 4 shows shading done with charcoal or pencil, Step 5 shows adding detail using a pen or a brush.

5. You can also add details with a pen, indicating scales and texture with strokes and cross-hatching.

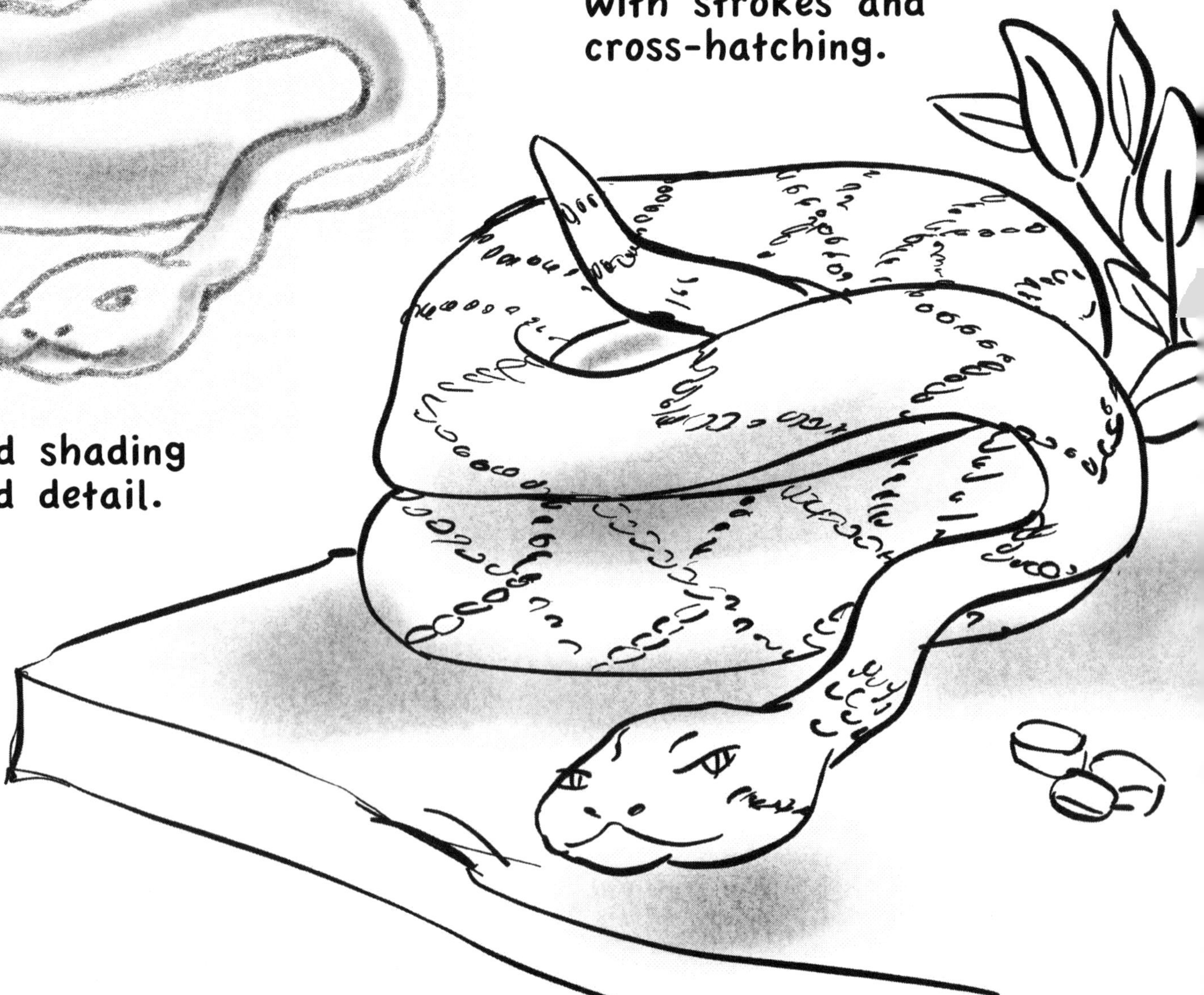

4. Add shading and detail.

Practice Page

Look at the page on the left. Draw the animal in the frame below, by following the steps listed.

RHINO

1. Draw the rhino's head.

2. Add an outline of the body.

3. Finish the drawing by adding the rest of the body and legs.

80

Practice Page

Look at the page on the left. Draw the animal in the frame below, by following the steps listed.

RHINO

The next steps can be used interchangeably to show more realism and detail in your drawings. We recommend using either one or the other. However sometimes you can combine the two. Step 4 shows shading done with charcoal or pencil, Step 5 shows adding detail using a pen or a brush.

4. Add shading and detail.

5. You can also add details with a pen, indicating skin texture with strokes and cross hatching.

Practice Page

Look at the page on the left. Draw the animal in the frame below, by following the steps listed.

PEACOCK

1. Draw the peacock's head.

2. Add an outline of the body.

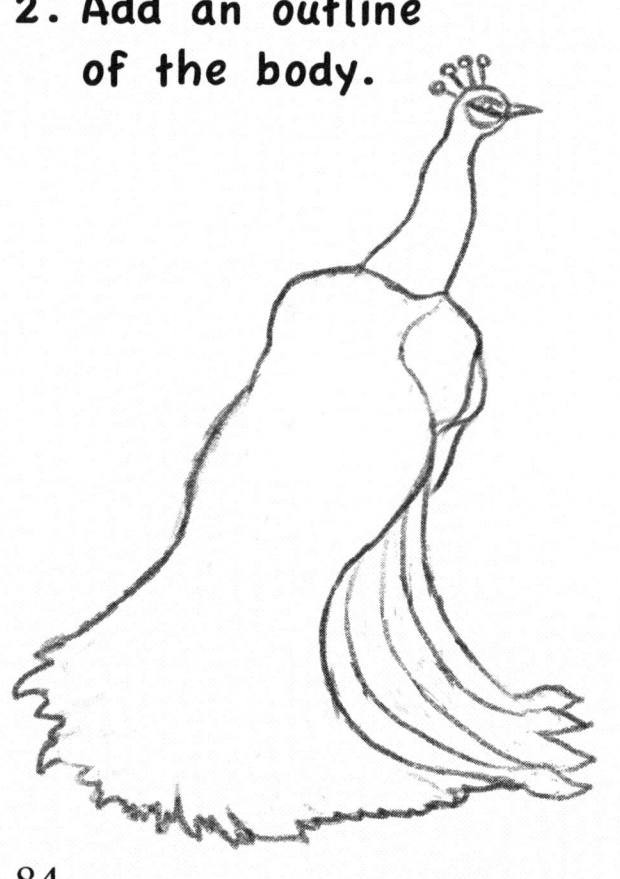

3. Finish the drawing by adding the feather details.

Practice Page

Look at the page on the left. Draw the animal in the frame below, by following the steps listed.

PEACOCK

The next steps can be used interchangeably to show more realism and detail in your drawings. We recommend using either one or the other. However sometimes you can combine the two. Step 4 shows shading done with charcoal or pencil, Step 5 shows adding detail using a pen or a brush.

4. Add shading and detail.

5. You can also add details with a pen, indicating feathers and texture, with strokes and crosshatching.

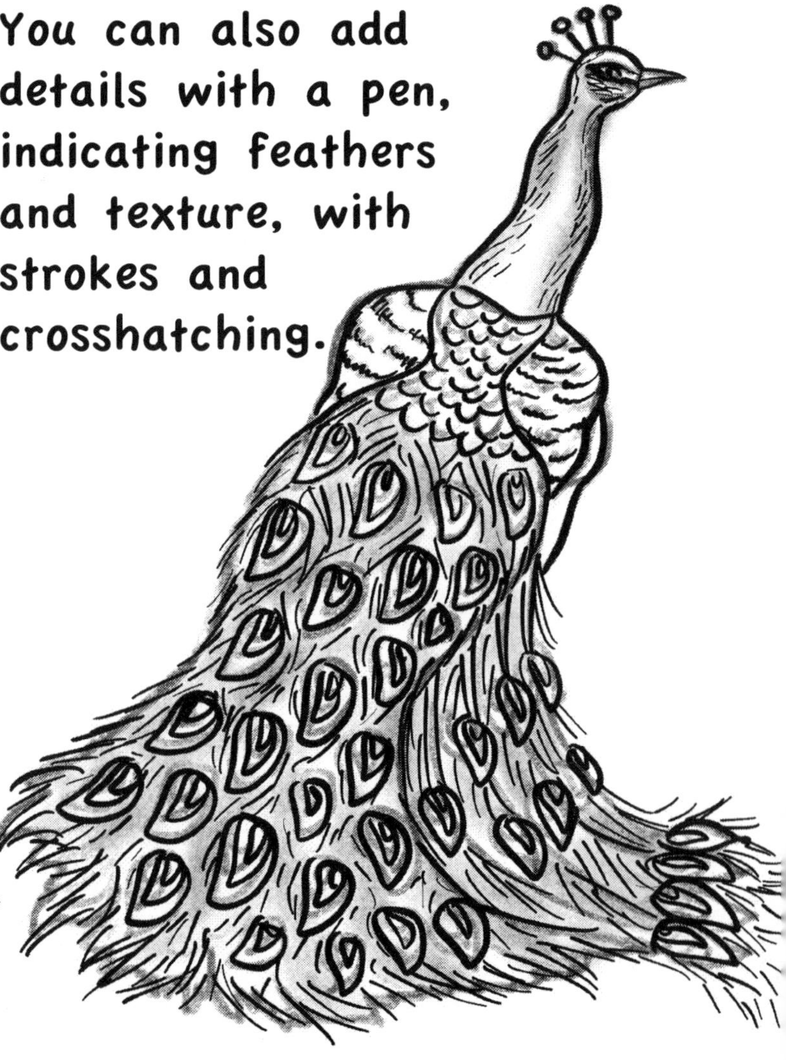

Practice Page

Look at the page on the left. Draw the animal in the frame below, by following the steps listed.

OSTRICH

1. Draw the ostrich's head.

2. Add an outline of the body.

3. Finish the drawing by adding the rest of the body, wings and legs.

Practice Page

Look at the page on the left. Draw the animal in the frame below, by following the steps listed.

OSTRICH

The next steps can be used interchangeably to show more realism and detail in your drawings. We recommend using either one or the other. However sometimes you can combine the two. Step 4 shows shading done with charcoal or pencil, Step 5 shows adding detail using a pen or a brush.

5. You can also add details with a pen, indicating feathers, with strokes and crosshatching.

4. Add shading and detail.

90

Practice Page

Look at the page on the left. Draw the animal in the frame below, by following the steps listed.

MONKEY

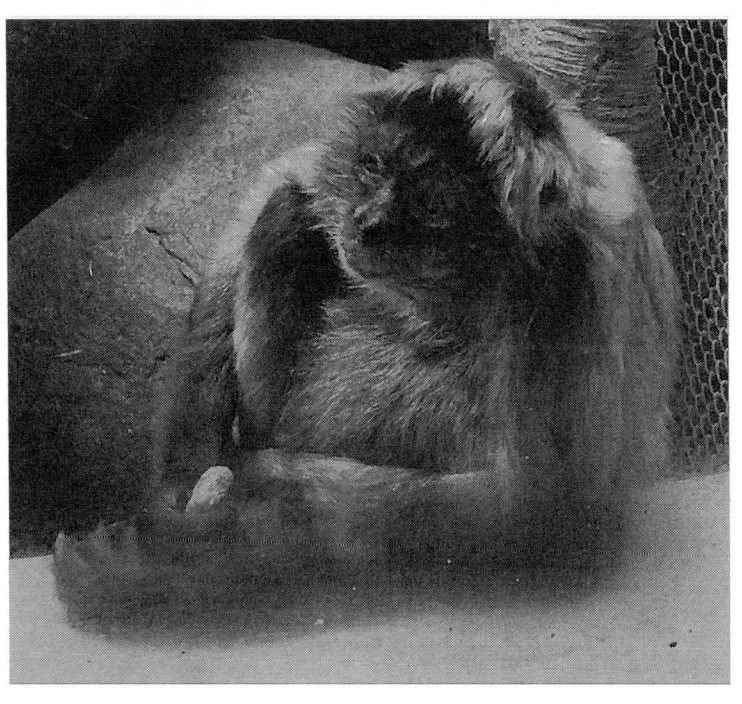

1. Draw the monkey's head.

2. Add an outline of the body.

3. Finish the drawing by adding the rest of the body and legs.

Practice Page

Look at the page on the left. Draw the animal in the frame below, by following the steps listed.

MONKEY

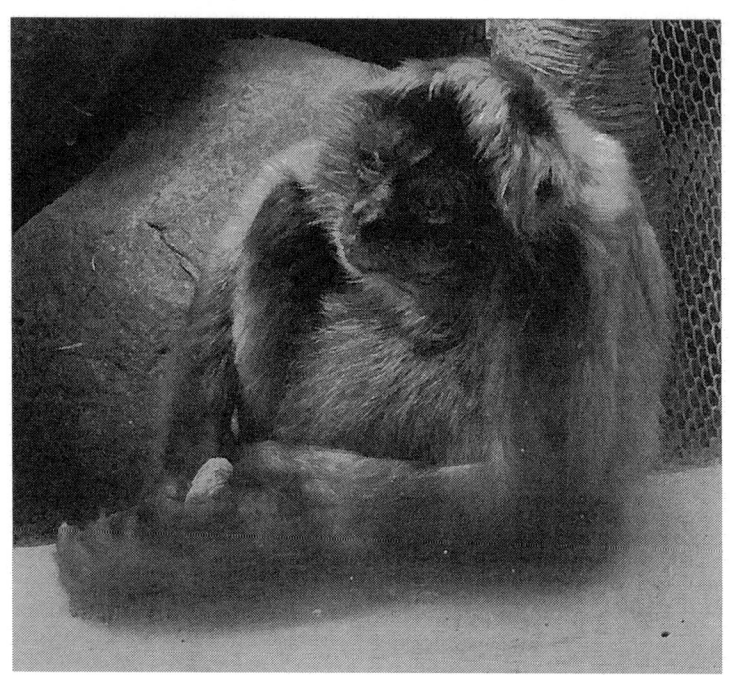

The next steps can be used interchangeably to show more realism and detail in your drawings. We recommend using either one or the other. However sometimes you can combine the two. Step 4 shows shading done with charcoal or pencil, Step 5 shows adding detail using a pen or a brush.

5. You can also add details with a pen, indicating hair and texture, with strokes and crosshatching.

4. Add shading and detail.

Practice Page

Look at the page on the left. Draw the animal in the frame below, by following the steps listed.

LLAMA

1. Draw the llama's head.

2. Add an outline of the body.

3. Finish the drawing by adding the rest of the body and legs.

Practice Page

Look at the page on the left. Draw the animal in the frame below, by following the steps listed.

LLAMA

The next steps can be used interchangeably to show more realism and detail in your drawings. We recommend using either one or the other. However sometimes you can combine the two. Step 4 shows shading done with charcoal or pencil, Step 5 shows adding detail using a pen or a brush.

5. You can also add details with a pen, indicating hair and details, with strokes and crosshatching.

4. Add shading and detail.

Practice Page

Look at the page on the left. Draw the animal in the frame below, by following the steps listed.

LEOPARD

1. Draw the leopard's head.

2. Add an outline of the body.

3. Finish the drawing by adding the rest of the body and legs.

100

Practice Page

Look at the page on the left. Draw the animal in the frame below, by following the steps listed.

101

LEOPARD

The next steps can be used interchangeably to show more realism and detail in your drawings. We recommend using either one or the other. However sometimes you can combine the two. Step 4 shows shading done with charcoal or pencil, Step 5 shows adding detail using a pen or a brush.

5. You can also add details with a pen, indicating fur and spots with strokes and crosshatching.

4. Add shading and detail.

Practice Page

Look at the page on the left. Draw the animal in the frame below, by following the steps listed.

103

KANGAROO

1. Draw the kangaroo's head.

2. Add an outline of the body.

3. Finish the drawing by adding the rest of the body and legs.

Practice Page

Look at the page on the left. Draw the animal in the frame below, by following the steps listed.

KANGAROO

The next steps can be used interchangeably to show more realism and detail in your drawings. We recommend using either one or the other. However sometimes you can combine the two. Step 4 shows shading done with charcoal or pencil, Step 5 shows adding detail using a pen or a brush.

4. Add shading and detail.

5. You can also add details with a pen, indicating fur and details with strokes and crosshatching.

Practice Page

Look at the page on the left. Draw the animal in the frame below, by following the steps listed.

Final Note

Thank you so much for drawing all of the fun animals in this book! This was a beginning for you to practice drawing animals from observation.

The ultimate way for you to learn to draw animals, is to draw them from life. Good tools to use are pencils of different softness and thickness, charcoal sticks and erasers. Once you have developed some confidence in your art, you can start to use disposable ink pens and pens where you can change out the cartridges.

Try to draw what you see. If you have domestic animals, draw them. You can also take a trip to the zoo and draw zoo animals. If you do not have access to seeing live animals, you can draw from videos or photos as well.

Once you have learned to draw most animals from observation, the next step is developing your own imagination, where you can draw animal characters based on real life, but adding your own spin on them, by making them more interesting and animated.

The most important thing for you to remember is to have fun when you draw and to not be afraid to mess up!

To begin sketching on your own, you can use some of the pages at the back of the paperback version of this book. You can also get a thick sketchbook at a discount store or an art store (many have a good sale section), and fill it up with your sketches of animals!

If you liked this book, please take a moment to leave a review on Amazon! Reviews help to make more great books for you to enjoy!

Also, if you enjoyed this book's style of teaching, you will love the rest of the books in our How To Draw series, which can be found on Amazon and other online retailers.

Practice Page

Use these pages to draw your own animals, either from life or the references you find.

Practice Page

Use these pages to draw your own animals, either from life or the references you find.

Practice Page

Use these pages to draw your own animals, either from life or the references you find.

112

Practice Page

Use these pages to draw your own animals, either from life or the references you find.

Practice Page

Use these pages to draw your own animals, either from life or the references you find.

Practice Page

Use these pages to draw your own animals, either from life or the references you find.

Practice Page

Use these pages to draw your own animals, either from life or the references you find.

116

Practice Page

Use these pages to draw your own animals, either from life or the references you find.

Practice Page

Use these pages to draw your own animals, either from life or the references you find.

Practice Page

Use these pages to draw your own animals, either from life or the references you find.

Practice Page

Use these pages to draw your own animals, either from life or the references you find.

Practice Page

Use these pages to draw your own animals, either from life or the references you find.

Practice Page

Use these pages to draw your own animals, either from life or the references you find.

Practice Page

Use these pages to draw your own animals, either from life or the references you find.

Practice Page

Use these pages to draw your own animals, either from life or the references you find.

Practice Page

Use these pages to draw your own animals, either from life or the references you find.

Practice Page

Use these pages to draw your own animals, either from life or the references you find.

Practice Page

Use these pages to draw your own animals, either from life or the references you find.

Practice Page

Use these pages to draw your own animals, either from life or the references you find.

Practice Page

Use these pages to draw your own animals, either from life or the references you find.

Practice Page

Use these pages to draw your own animals, either from life or the references you find.

Practice Page

Use these pages to draw your own animals, either from life or the references you find.

Practice Page

Use these pages to draw your own animals, either from life or the references you find.

Practice Page

Use these pages to draw your own animals, either from life or the references you find.

Practice Page

Use these pages to draw your own animals, either from life or the references you find.

Practice Page

Use these pages to draw your own animals, either from life or the references you find.

Practice Page

Use these pages to draw your own animals, either from life or the references you find.

Practice Page

Use these pages to draw your own animals, either from life or the references you find.

Practice Page

Use these pages to draw your own animals, either from life or the references you find.

Practice Page

Use these pages to draw your own animals, either from life or the references you find.

Practice Page

Use these pages to draw your own animals, either from life or the references you find.

Practice Page

Use these pages to draw your own animals, either from life or the references you find.

Practice Page

Use these pages to draw your own animals, either from life or the references you find.

Practice Page

Use these pages to draw your own animals, either from life or the references you find.

Practice Page

Use these pages to draw your own animals, either from life or the references you find.

Practice Page

Use these pages to draw your own animals, either from life or the references you find.

Practice Page

Use these pages to draw your own animals, either from life or the references you find.

Practice Page

Use these pages to draw your own animals, either from life or the references you find.

Printed in Great Britain
by Amazon